AMERICAN LOTUS

poems by
Kevin Casey

Glass Lyre Press

Copyright © 2018 Kevin Casey
Paperback ISBN: 978-1-941783-49-8

All rights reserved: except for the purpose of quoting brief passages for review, no part of this book may be reproduced or transmitted in any form or by any means, electronic or mechanical, including photocopying, recording, or by any information storage and retrieval system, without permission in writing from the publisher.

Cover art: Chung Yin Eric Chan | Dreamstime.com
Author photo:
Design & layout: Steven Asmussen
Copyediting: Linda E. Kim

Glass Lyre Press, LLC
P.O. Box 2693
Glenview, IL 60025
www.GlassLyrePress.com

Contents

Acknowledgments   vii

I

American Lotus (*Nelumbo lutea*)	1
A Busy Mind	2
I Wrote this Note to You—	3
For Sale	4
Taking Down the Clothesline	5
Driving to Your Parents' for the Holidays	6
After the Accident	7
"I've got some bad news…"	8
Retread	9
Telegraph Poles	10
Vacation's End	11
A Wall of Photographs	12
Sorry to Part	13
Hancock Point, Early Autumn	14

A Week in the Back Bay	15
Ode to the Green Line, Coolidge Corner	16
Street Sweeper	18
Chesapeake and Ohio, Northbound	19

II

Carelessweed (*Amaranthus palmeri*)	23
Once, Driving to Work	24
The Office Scarecrow	25
Curating a Necktie Collection	26
A Captain of Industry Leaves the Firm	27
Fossilization	28
Trespassing	29
A New Confectionery	30
Nocturne with Worms	31
Christmas Cookies	32
Rediscovery	33
At the Halfway Mark	34
A Garage in Summer	35
Partridge Hunting	36
Clearing His Throat	37
Quartz	38

III

Red Maple (*Acer rubrum*)	41
Snake in Effigy	42
A Map of the Northern Cardinal's Range	43
A Stream in February	44
Snow Fence Sonnet	45
Snowmobiling at Midnight	46
Poem in Which My Vehicle is Mistaken for a Police Car	47

Street Signs	48
Northbound, Route 95	49
Evening on the Causeway	50
To a Mosquito	51
For a Misplaced Hatchet	52
A Trout in the Well	53
For a New Roof	54
Elegy for a Sapling in Three Revelations	55
Abandoned Bicycle	56
The Natural History of Stones	57
A Cemetery in Greene, Maine	58
Route 202, Heading North	59
About the Author	61

Acknowledgments

"American Lotus (*Nelumbo lutea*)" first appeared in *Olentangy Review*.
"A Busy Mind" first appeared in *Mud Season Review*.
"I Wrote this Note to You" first appeared in *Red Booth Review*.
"For Sale" first appeared in *Heyday Magazine*.
"Taking Down the Clothesline" first appeared in *Sourland Mountain Review*.
"Driving to Your Parents' for the Holidays" first appeared in *Leaves of Ink*.
"After the Accident" first appeared in *A Quiet Courage*.
"I've got some bad news…" first appeared in *Grasslimb*.
"Retread" first appeared in *Clear Poetry*.
"Telegraph Poles" first appeared in *The Corner Club Press*.
"Vacation's End" first appeared in *Ohio Edit*.
"A Wall of Photographs" first appeared in *Sun Star Review*.
"Sorry to Part first appeared in *Menacing Hedge*.
Hancock Point, Early Autumn" first appeared in *Three Monkeys Magazine*.
"A Week in the Back Bay" first appeared in *Amuse-Bouche (Lunch Ticket)*.
"Ode to the Green Line, Coolidge Corner" first appeared in *Ithaca Lit*.
"Street Sweeper" first appeared in *The Mondegreen*.
"Chesapeake and Ohio, Northbound" first appeared in *The Homestead Review*.
"Carelessweed (*Amaranthus palmeri*)" first appeared in *Bird's Thumb*.
"Once, Driving to Work" first appeared in *The Schuylkill Valley Journal*.
"The Office Scarecrow" first appeared in *Angle Poetry*.
"Curating a Necktie Collection" first appeared in *American Arts Quarterly*.
"A Captain of Industry Leaves the Firm" first appeared in *Mud Season Review*.
"Fossilization" first appeared in *Words Dance*.
"Trespassing" first appeared in *Sweet Tree Review*.
"Nocturne with Worms" first appeared in *Summerset Review*.
"Christmas Cookies" first appeared in *The Basil O'Flaherty*.
"At the Halfway Mark" first appeared in *Lost River*.
"A Garage in Summer" first appeared in *Sun Star Review*.
"Quartz" first appeared in *Inklette*.
"Red Maple (*Acer rubrum*)" first appeared in *Spry*.

"Snake in Effigy" first appeared in *The Maine Review*.

"A Map of the Northern Cardinal's Range" first appeared in *The Schuylkill Valley Journal*.

"A Stream in February" first appeared in *Triggerfish Critical Review*.

"Snow Fence Sonnet" first appeared in *The Basil O' Flaherty*.

"Poem in which my vehicle is mistaken for a police car" first appeared in *Roanoke Review*.

"Street Signs" first appeared in *Pittsburgh Poetry Houses*.

"Northbound, Route 95" first appeared in *Sourland Mountain Review*.

"Evening at the Causeway" first appeared in *Provo Canyon Review*.

"To a Mosquito" first appeared in *Sourland Mountain Review*.

"For a Misplaced Hatchet" first appeared in *Switchback*.

"A Trout in the Well" first appeared in *Sourland Mountain Review*.

"For a New Roof" first appeared in *Split Rock Review*.

"Elegy for a Sapling in Three Revelations" first appeared in *The Hollins Critic*.

"A Cemetery in Greene, Maine" first appeared in *Ohio Edit*.

"Route 202, Heading West" first appeared in *Glassworks*.

I

American Lotus (*Nelumbo Lutea*)

In a cove away from the sunny buttons
of the bullhead lilies, their cream and pearl crowns
fold themselves into the shape of a tear
each day before nightfall.   With their coterie
of stars reflected in the water
about them, each blossom has risen
on its thin stem from the lake bottom's mud
like a dream of a moon it's never seen.

A Busy Mind

The knob on the old truck's radio
is a spigot to fill the cab with shapes
and patterns, and rinse away the thoughts
of a busy mind. A hundred miles north,
the signal thins to a trickle, a whispered
tissue of static decaying unnoticed
by slow degrees, like the day now ground
to a granular twilight. Another hour,
and the radio has dried to sparse clicks;
what light remains has narrowed to the road's
center line unreeling into the emptiness,
with nothing but a busy mind to flood
the valley on the far side of this high notch.

I Wrote this Note to You—

on paper made
of a lake bed

dried by stars,
planed smooth
by the moon.

The pen nib
was whittled
from a passing gale,

and the ink
a jar of starlings,
swirling, iridescent
in the glass's curl.

But folded,
crease over crease,
the note never narrows,

the knife-neat pleating
won't ease these
vexing edges,

and so the envelope waits—
patient, blameless.

For Sale

To see a *For Sale* sign leaning toward you
in the windshield of a jeep as you drive by
on your way to work—a candy apple
ornament waiting on someone's lawn.

And to mean to stop each afternoon
for five days straight, but to continue north
neither tired, nor anxious to be home—
only an upended hubcap emptied

of desire, somehow a different man
with the sun in your left eye, and the jeep's
coat of dust and pollen pocked and cratered
by the dew as it pooled and dried.

Taking Down the Clothesline

A half dozen years ago, you had said
you wanted to see laundry billowing,
old-fashioned and shining against the green
of the yard when you woke in the morning.

But the line I fastened to the tree out back,
looped around pulleys, its tightener
like a zinc fist riding along its length,
was rarely used that first year, then not again.

Jeans and pillow cases would sour
after days of rain, and you couldn't wait
for the washer's water to sublimate
from shirts hanging stiff in the winter wind.

Mostly it stretched from the lipped ridges
of the boxelder's wounds to the porch
for the benefit of tired swallows--
a taut and silent telephone line.

When I finally cut that cord, sawed through
its cotton with a kitchen knife, the tree
seemed relieved, and the house and myself
regained our balance with the guyline gone,
no longer pulled toward that pretense.

Driving to Your Parents' for the Holidays

We marked the spot in the loden sky
where the sun should have been—
driving north along the road's cracked tongue,
dry despite the rain the dawn had staunched.
Our words were a frail scaffolding

of cane and rush to brace civility,
courteous phrases filling in spaces,
falling and rising with the radio's
rambling, neutral testimony.

Through the slag piles of motels and gas stations,
gray-bricked, neon-smeared, past mute traffic lights
that mouthed no warnings, the car dragged along
beyond the city's bitter breath, beyond
the pale afternoon, each staring ahead
at our own horizon. Their fist of driveway
reached from its roots to pull us toward
the commotion and the misplaced care
of that house, into the waking for what
had finally expired on our drive north.

After the Accident

The policeman sweeps up
shards of red and yellow plastic
and safety glass nuggets
that shimmer in the dawn—
confetti from a piñata
once the party is over,
and the ambulance
has driven away.

"I've got some bad news…"

And then the way your voice
broke on the phone—
the sea floor fracturing,

and waves pouring through;
the green swells emptied,
plunging, until the stars

themselves must cling to
the night's cold net to
save themselves, helpless.

Retread

Southbound, chasing mirages that ebb
like waves of mercury—a black form blossoms
to the right of the broken center line's semaphore.
It might have been a skunk or porcupine
before it paid that final toll, but closer, its edges
flare like wingtips poised in a parody of flight,
and so it was perhaps a raven or a crow
whose blasé gait was just a single hop too slow.
But closer still it shows itself instead to be a scrap
of retread, remains of a tire shredded and discarded—
never living, yet no less lifeless—a relic dejected
and framed in my rear view mirror, diminishing.

Telegraph Poles

once lined this dusty road,
and as their barkless boles
withered to the dirt,
their glass and ceramic seeds—
rain-rinsed, glowing green,
white and blue—grew
to ranks of telephone poles
in furrows along the asphalt,
grew fat on our chatter
and half again as tall
as their stunted forebears,
undernourished as these were,
on their diet of dots and dashes.

Vacation's End

First, you'll lose track of the date,
and then the days, and finally—
unhitched from any purpose—
you'll judge each morning only by its weather.

But if you wake to find slate clouds
moored in your postcard harbor,
you'll take an aimless, rainy drive inland,
leave the salt smell and the townies

placed to decorate the wharfs and quays,
and wander off that postcard
beyond the bell buoy's warning,
into other people's workweeks—

past charmless convenience stores,
planned housing tracts, strip malls
and the trash cans that guard the driveway,
and a lawnmower left out in the yard.

And puzzled as to what these people do
all day and why, you'll head back to the harbor,
trying to find the postcard's edge as you
begin to worry how tall your lawn has grown.

A Wall of Photographs

Dusting the wooden edges and cardboard backs
of all these hanging photographs, I can cite
the dates and places where I took them,
though only because I recognize
the background waterfall, the beach hut,
the ages of my children trapped in glass.

But I can't recall the sun on my arms,
the low tide's sulphur bite, or the arrangement
of desires and fears that formed the composition
of those days.
                    If I could somehow
burnish these brown fiber boards to a smooth
translucence, I might look from their angle
and see who these people smiled at years ago—
a shadow enclosing moments in his lens,
a silhouette unframed, fixed yet missing.

Sorry to Part

We met again in
this poverty of time,

beneath fractured hills
and the black, jagged

line of spruce,
where the north wind

entwined us in sheer,
glaucous ribbons,

and the sun
scraped its thin arc

above the pewter lake.
My memory

of your leaving
was made of a moment

in the curved,
dry rib of that place.

Hancock Point, Early Autumn

The swells that breathe about the wharf
untangle mats of sea wrack, and the land breeze
sorts out strands of brackish fume.

Three sailboats anchor the horizon,
and the day, splayed across the September sea,
gnaws and cracks the marrowless sun.

Our season weakens; soon its weather
will bruise the sea with shoals of listing clouds.
Autumn is a bleached whelk chrysalis,

a mermaid's purse of brine and bone,
where memory founders, and the dipping tern
dreams of sleep between the furrowed waves.

A Week in the Back Bay

We wandered your city
for five days, hemmed within
those same cobbled creases,
tucked between brownstones—
mordant lines grown soft
in the damp October night.

As the slow, sibilant traffic
parted for us with lumbering grace,
we streamed through the darkness,
faces pearlescent, strung together
in shadow, flowing into
patient, silent homes,
or hidden cafes carved
into sheer cliff sides.

Children of green steel trestles
and granite curbing, unwearied—
my vision fails before the end
of your wharves and spires
that stretch beyond
the sharp exhaust of idling taxis,
and bleared lights
that sting the wet asphalt.

What is it you see among
these crumbling abutments
and slabs of crooked concrete
shelved against the silhouettes
of trees that drip and quiver against
the chain-links and brick?
What words form for you
in this dim language,
dissolved and dank beneath
these watery lights pooling?

Ode to the Green Line, Coolidge Corner

I.

I have traced my daily circuit past
unnumbered spurs and sidings, walked a path
plaited with those made by these countless forms,
these ghosts with their vacant, aimless faces.

Shadows of stairwells and window casings
are scabbed onto brown and gray storefronts
receding, shiplapped into the background,
abiding in the blurred periphery
as the darkness settles.

II.

The tower's clock is of no account—
its luminous face static, ungauging.
But from my bench I see the light rail
streaming up the boulevard, marking distance
and time, linking another afternoon

to the evening's quiet easement; clacking
past these stunted trees, the placarded
capsules flow—a jade-skirted chaplet
strung along a catenary wire—
to meet with me again.

III.

And having reached our destination,
we pause in the wake of the hollow whistle
of its brakes, billowing out beyond
the crosswalks and the streetlights igniting.

In this pantograph of sidewalk and rails,
joined in this symmetry of transit,
we write these city blocks each day
in our straight and shared calligraphy.

Street Sweeper

Fairfield Street, Boston, 2003

Backed into their corrugated caves, the plow trucks
hibernate, and now the street sweeper has returned

from its slow migration, crawling like a marigold snail
beneath my half-opened sash. When winter had grown

out of its charm, its midnight storms magnified
our isolation, and we waited for the rumbling

scythe to glide through the boulevard, its low lullabye
echoing along the brownstones, clearing away

the burden of our separate solitudes. The sand
it scattered never seemed to measure up to much

until the rains came, and the storm drains grew choked
with rivers of silt. Inside, little changed with the seasons—

the tilt of morning light across the paths we wore
throughout these rooms, the tapping of the radiator's

cryptic code grown fitful, then silent. You left to make
your own way long before the sweeper returned,
tracing waves of scoured pavement in its wake.

Chesapeake and Ohio, Northbound

These towns and cities will hide their rail lines,
drown them beneath some outskirt's shore running
the length of a hundred gasping years:
chain-linked lots guard blossoming slag piles,

the back ends of boarding houses, clothes lines,
fire escapes and cinderblock shacks all
immersed in the smell of grease and waste oil,
tires smoldering just beyond the neon.

Even the edges of feed corn fields
hide half-rusted barrels heeled into the dirt
between stacks of forsaken crossties
sulking in their creosote shadows.

Clattering south of Baltimore last night,
past bricked up windows and sagging power lines,
I took with me to sleep the image
of children's faces lit by a pallet fire.

Another dawn in a different state bobs
to the surface, soaked through but breathing—
frail light caresses graffiti that seeps
up the sides of box cars like water damage.

II

Carelessweed (*Amaranthus palmeri*)

Cultivated for food before the ships
    and horses came, it now grows six feet tall

between the cotton rows, and poisonous
    with our fertilizers, whorling heavenward

in volutions of deep-veined leaves whose size
    decrease, receding finally to the spire

of its pale inflorescence—its only care
    in the world to grow closer to the sky.

Once, Driving to Work

Each day I drove past the final black line
of trees down into the valley of my workday—
the river that curls itself across its floor
concealed beneath the residue of night.
Now running late and the seasons changing,
the sky behind me glowed bronze,
burnished by the sun still unseen.
Miles across the valley, the same shadowed
smokestack waited like a sundial's gnomon
to measure out the day's every moment.

But the braided fists of smoke that slipped
from its mouth toward the lingering stars
glowed gold, caught in the day's first light.
And in that numinous moment before dawn,
the valley was flooded with a peace beyond
all labor and care, the world suspended
in an instant of becoming that was so pure
I could lay down even the obligation of hope.

The Office Scarecrow

And I will fashion a scarecrow inside
this conference room, lash it firm to this
vinyl chair with course lengths of sisal twine.
And it will sit in my stead, transcribing

empty notes on splayed corn husks, silent
in its wisdom, patient and resolute—
a steadfast fixture of the company.
The gourd for a head will sit at a slant,

showing interest and concern in equal,
judicious measure, while the rush-stuffed vest
conveys to all its corpulent success.
And when it begins to rot and decay

by degrees, slow fiscal year after year,
the slouched attitude, slump and bleeding stain
will mark only the accumulating
burdens of obligation and of care.

And I will happily trade places
with this counterfeit, and spend my days
pegged to a field, taking counsel with the crows
in the still, easy hours at day's end.

Curating a Necktie Collection

You'll note how this one wreathes about the neck,
the paisleys swirling in their burgundy curves
like clove smoke, evoking Victorian
authority. Careless fiber pairings
may promote a slackened attitude—
the fussy swatch of a maiden aunt's couch.

The fish thorn stitch of this knitted model
conveys its crafted insouciance through
the threads that add a softened, rutted note
and a homespun blur to the sharpened lines
of a button-down's starch-soaked warp and weft,

while the emerald polygons of that cravat
are crystalline nuclei shimmering,
that shun all scrutiny as they index
the trajectory of stars within their calm
geometry. The fractals blossoming
in the sheen of its silk edges, ground keen,
gleam like smoldering phosphorus along
the length of that alchemical vector.

And this limp bouquet on the valet stand,
these silk and cotton strands, comprise a rare
menagerie of slender beasts—half albatross,
half tail-eating snake. You'll note, at last,
the way each calculates and measures out
my workdays like a scrupulous fabric rule.

A Captain of Industry Leaves the Firm

*"Out of sight of land the sailor feels safe.
It is the beach that worries him." —Charles G. Davis*

Sitting adjacent at the boardroom table,
I saw the hole in the old man's sock
just above his wingtip's stern—a porthole
into a humanity hidden beneath
all the briefings and variance reports,
showing flesh that was not unlike my own,
and so I was glad to have come aboard.

When he grew ill the following year,
the treatments left his skin a seasick green
the color of sky before a waterspout
touches down. The last time I saw him,
he was sitting in his navy blue suit
on an island of lawn outside the office
building, leaning against a Chinaberry tree.

Though his face glowed in the late morning sun,
chartless and foundered, his eyes were no longer
fixed upon the horizon, but on his hands
listing on his thighs, the runaway line
of his workday having stolen through his grip.

Fossilization

Our blood-soaked bones
grow fossilized at night;

while we sleep,
something particulate,
suspended, seeps
through membranes,

settles deep
within those posts and knobs
of gleaming ivory.

The soft, surrounding
tissues ossify,
calcified deposits
sprout and bloom

in organs, spread
their chalky webs until
we're statuesque, inured.

And then it's just the waiting
for erosion's slow exposure,
the sweep and chip
of brush and pick:

cataloged and set
in some eventual display,
we're cordoned off
by stanchions of brass
and velvet rope.

Trespassing

Where the wire fence meets the pointed slats
of a wood stockade, a rusted corner
dog-eared by the weight of thirty years
of children.
              From their tireless migrations
across back-to-back suburban yards,
rutted trails weave behind garden sheds
and rows of ornamental cedars—

caution bends the only curves in their straight
line to the five and dime, avoiding dogs
and wives in bathrobes who scold from back porches.

Guiltless animals relentless and convinced
of the logic in their geometry,
they practice trespassing on weekends
and after school, for now their only concept
of property confined to the paper bag
each culprit clutches, filled with candy.

A New Confectionery

Perforated candy boxes torn topless,
red, green and yellow, displayed on angled shelves—
even ranks and rows that sugared the aisle air
between the canned goods and cleaning supplies.

But my fifty cents misplaced, I was halfway
across the parking lot empty-handed
before another boy ran toward me
from the store: *The man at the register said
he thought you'd taken something—what'd you steal?*

Frozen on the blacktop, heat rising
to my face, I finally turned away
from the store and the boy's admiring smile—
a fresh exile left to make his way home

through the woods and contemplate this new
confectionery: the sour taste
of grown-up outrage and indignation,
and infamy, surprisingly sweet.

Nocturne with Worms

The night before each fishing trip,
his father let him stay up
later than the sun so the yard
might steep in dew and darkness,
and the worms might rise and stretch
themselves across the grass—
coral tassels glistening singly,
or entwined in a braid made
iridescent by their flashlight.

Long after, it wasn't the boat's
motor tremoring in the dawn,
nor the biddable sunfish
he sought to recall, but those
warm nights and the glint
of twilit life that slipped
from his hands like quicksilver,
draining through hidden holes
back into the earth.

Christmas Cookies

We had forgotten the Christmas cookies
left entombed within their festive tin
atop the fridge—out of sight and mind,
and now March already upon us.

The round lid rolled away, the ginger snaps,
buckeyes, and pale flesh of sugar cookies
had remained whole, decors and nonpareils
left clinging where impatient children sowed them.

But none will risk this spritz cookie Eucharist,
the butter and sugar incarnations
of that season grown stale and suspect.
The children have since moved on to the feast

of chocolate and jellybeans, and the less young
among us are glad to set faith aside,
and to welcome the spring's more certain
sacrament of reconciliation.

Rediscovery

With each new season, she would come
sweeping up the stairs like a current,
carrying armfuls of impractical flotsam—
decorative elements forever upwelling
from the cellar: the painted milkcan
bristling with moneyplants and rushes,
the stoneware jugs run aground
in empty parlor corners, a cobalt
vase stranded atop the bookcase,
and wreaths of grapevine and bittersweet
left high and dry beside the porchlight.
And with the cold weather, boxes
of glass and tin baubles would rise
like bubbles from the basement.

By the time she was fifty, her husband
had lined two walls beneath the house
with shelves for her china bowls,
her candlesticks and bookends.
And as the years coated this collection
in silted layers of nostalgia
and forgetfulness, she would spend
more time below the bright commotion
of her home, exploring the steel and pine
plank racks that sat exposed
like the rent hull of a foundered ship,
delighting in the rediscovery
of all these sunken treasures.

At the Halfway Mark

Weaving my middle-aged way through these streets
on my pre-dawn jog, I know the houses
along this colorless route less by their
shadowed mass and geometry—the outline
of their angled attics, jet ranks of windows
that might place a pale rhombus on the lawn—

and more by the air they leak into the street:
a drier rumbling its floral notes along
a driveway, the smell of breakfast flowing
from a screen door. And at my route's midpoint,
the stately house they've chosen to deconstruct
and not demolish—its roof removed
like a spice jar lid, the sweetness of dry-rot
and hemlock sap unraveling heavenward
from the loom of studs left standing in the dark,
each day pry bars and sledges pulling the house
closer to its granite stones. It seemed a disgrace
to watch such a grand building lowered
by degrees, its usefulness long since paid out.

But as my path wound around the corner
toward home, I paused on creaking knees
at this halfway mark, a mist of sweat rising,
and wondered if I was winding my way
or unwinding, gathering up or becoming undone,
the house and myself left sighing in the twilight.

A Garage in Summer

The shrill buzz of cicadas would send
my grandparents sheltering from the heat
to lawnchairs in the darkened doorway
of their garage. And from that cave they watched
us play hopscotch and jumprope on the tongue
of hot tar that lolled out to the road.

We had grown out of those games and toys
by the time our grandfather died, although
grandmother still whiled away her summer days
in the mouth of the garage, her form
dissolving into its cool shadows
as the afternoons settled to evening,
and the radiance of the cicadas' call
dimmed to the crickets' furtive glimmer.

Partridge Hunting

We walked along the stream into a field
that bristled with small spruce, while the sun
lingered on its perch atop the mountains
to the east. Two abreast, our shotguns
pointed into the wood-reed like oars.
In the grainy air, the shape in the branches
might have been a porcupine or twigs
tangled into a witch's broom. Our minds
drew out a partridge neck from the downy mass
that bobbed and dipped, then dissolved into nothing
as we waited, whispering. Barrels raised
and lowered, and raised again. Finally,
the top half of that form turned like a turret
as the sun stirred the waves of seed heads,
and we saw the white mask and onyx depths
of a saw-whet owl's eyes. And from the twilight
of that cool morning we crafted our account,
to the score of the stream and the wind through
sage-green needles, of how that beautiful thing
was saved, and we its rescuers, and how
that autumn day was ripe and heavy
like the game bags at our backs, filled by noon
with its own pinioned softness grown cold,
and eyes dull slits that stared into nothing.

Clearing His Throat

He'd been gone almost a year when I saw
my sister again at Thanksgiving.
As we caught up over coffee she said,
The way you coughed just then sounded like Dad.
Mine was a common allergic reaction
that I'd carried since childhood, bundled
with its matching sneeze. His was a quarrel
he'd begun with his Luckies when they first
came to loggerheads at the age of fourteen.

But how fitting that two people—who
for fifty years spoke languages wholly
foreign to each other, down to each sputtered
syllable and their rising, colliding
intonations—should finally come to share
at most this rasping, meaningless gesture.
And how comforting he should speak through me
with no more than this harmless *ahem*,
this courteous request for attention.

Quartz

For years we kept the quartz stones you found,
placed them in rows upon the windowsills
of your room like teeth along a weathered jaw.

After a spring rain in the garden,
past the wood chips at the playground's edge,
at the gravel inlet of our driveway,

you'd rush to seize each alabaster knot,
as if it might sink back under the soil—
the bedrock rippling with that milky droplet.

Obvious and common, its hold on you
was charming, although I was the one
to ferry your finds, happy to bear
the clattering pull of full pockets.

Our last good hunt before the snow,
we walked the bank of a late fall stream—
two bundled figures floating above
the cobbles like frozen smoke, our bodies
nearly translucent in the clear autumn air.

III

Red Maple (*Acer rubrum*)

Rocking in the tides of wind that swell
above the canopy, the red maple
was felled weeks ago, plunging with a sigh
as the earth rushed up to receive it.

Removed from its roots, capillaries
cauterized by the heat of the chainsaw's bar,
that length of bark and bole, though lowered
to its hands and knees, has yet to touch the ground.

And the buds that February dipped
in claret have somehow fledged, new flesh
hanging from the tip of every twig,
as if the maple had been trimmed from this life

without knowing, lingering in the shade
with all the world turned upon its side.

Snake in Effigy

A milkweed stalk was caught in our neighbor's
   late summer maple bucking and splitting,
      bark-snagged and toppled with the rest

of the quartered logs in the four cords
   left in my dooryard, waiting to be stacked
      once the mornings grew chill and hatchet sharp.

And finding that stem as I filled the shed—
   now black and wreathed about the logs—
      I jumped back, startled at this vague suggestion

of a snake, though the ground was hard,
   and I knew their kind were trussed and torpid,
      tucked away among the roots for months to come—

except, it would seem, for the few cool loops
   I keep coiled around my mind, sheltered
      from the north wind, to warm and quicken my blood.

A Map of the Northern Cardinal's Range

A wave of Prussian blue
the color of the shadows
we're washed in
these winter mornings
rises north along
the map, only to ebb
before my county's coast,
and so no cardinal will ever come.

But framed by the kitchen window,
the apples still hang
cat-faced and sallow,
anxious for a flash
of that black mask,
and the flick and snap
of a rose madder cassock.

A Stream in February

The snow beneath the alders tightens
at the bank to glazed plates
of pewter, cyan and white
where ice has grown
to hide the black warp
of winter water, and coat the beam
of shale ledge over which
the freshet's selvedge edge unfolds.

One small tear remains
amidstream the stillness—
and through this gap,
beads simmer on the verge,
and are pulled away
or escape into the frozen air
in a mist that rises skyward,
entwined with the sound
of the stream's constant weaving.

Snow Fence Sonnet

By a trick of your position,
it seems to pay out along
the landscape from the barn door's mouth
like a song of twisted wire
and rough-milled slats of aspen—
lonely notes on a listing staff.
Both the barn and fence stain the hill
above the pines with the same tone
of old blood, the same rose hue
of a near-spent coal releasing
its slow heat, and the snow whirls
and dances about the fence's
boney knees as it marches across
these quiet drifts toward spring.

Snowmobiling at Midnight

We met by the gas station beneath
a moon near full but distant as a star,
and across the scattered lattice of maple
shadows it cast, I followed him, pulled
through our exhaust into the small, blue hours.

Having traveled this far into most nights,
I'd be sifting through the strange narrative
of dreams, but now we skimmed at highway speeds
along a rutted track—ghosts falling aimless
through the indigo, just a breath away
from trees streaming past in a watery blur.

My tired mind lay curled head to tail
inside the cushion of my helmet.
Lulled and squinting, I followed the bleared eye
of red tail light that wavered before me
in time with my motor's hum, like some
memory fluttering just beyond reach.

And on the final loop, when the trail arced
around the base of a hill, there was a light
as bright as day—a midnight groomer,
its blade slicing the trail smooth, descending
the ridge on its massive tracks like an angel,
and the woods flooded with its brilliance.

Pulled over, blinking at the spectacle,
I strained to hear the voice of Gabriel
above its engine, to learn what these visions
of the last two-hundred miles had meant,
and to know whether any dawn would come.

Poem in Which My Vehicle is Mistaken for a Police Car

The government plates on this state college car
lend more authority than either myself
or this old Crown Vic deserve, yet I'll take
this borrowed thrill and ply my way along
the southbound stream, worrying the eighteen-wheelers—
lumbering whales with pickups and box trucks
hurrying in their wake like unweaned calves—

and I'll chasten to the point of braking
these schools of coupes and hatchbacks that flash
their tail lights in warning to others of their kind:
a shark now swims among them, for at least
the next three exits—a streak of unmarked
ivory behind a black-tipped snout,
patrolling this jersey barrier reef.

STREET SIGNS

Pausing at these corners, we strain
over steering wheels to read the signs
of flightless birds confined and flat
upon their posts, perched in plumes
of green and white. And somehow,
in this poor augury, we hope to learn
from them which path to take,
although they've never flown a foot
along their namesakes' way.

Northbound, Route 95

Boat on the highway,
white propeller blades
struggling to turn
in the gliding trailer's wake—
   a shore-stranded fish
      mouthing arid syllables
         in its agony of thirst.

Evening on the Causeway

The telephone line that parts the eastern sky
above the causeway is trimmed with a valance
of neon bobbers and spoons slick with chrome,
shot-baubled filaments and lures spangled
and hanging in display as if to dry.

Summer evenings after dinner, the gravel road
below is lined with old men and young families
sitting on lawn chairs and coolers to watch
the tips of fishing rods pierce the setting sun.

And in those few minutes before the cars
are loaded up, that curtain of tackle
ignites as it catches the last rays of light
and shines above their heads—each careless
cast and dangling misjudgment now forgiven.

To a Mosquito

Resting on the porch table, rear legs raised,
your belly droops with a salty dollop
of someone's blood—mine perhaps, siphoned
through insensate ankle skin, or my child's,
and so mine by extension, though perhaps
a thinner brine drawn from a dog or deer.

With the sunset behind you, your decanted
treasure glows, carmine and translucent,
and assuming you could rise, so blood-drunk
and weighted down, I would spare both your life
and an evening of itching to watch a flock
of your irksome kind, each ferrying a drop
of me across the yard like fireflies—
dull lanterns in the dusk shuttling warmth
instead of light above the dew-cooled field.

For a Misplaced Hatchet

The metronome of its ashen handle
counted time against my thigh as I walked,
but at some point it stopped, and I did not.

A half hour's search among the poplars
to the north of the pasture, then darkness
drove me home, and so there it remains.

Once the sun had chopped it free from the snow
that spring, flattened shoots of irises grew
about it in a fence, and the damp breath

of soil etched fissures in its lacquer.
Its polished face reflected the flickering
pulse of day and night, until a fretwork

of rust was cut across its mirror,
and warm rains sought to wash it into the mold
as it turned from tool to artefact.

These reveries grow more vivid as it
settles into its bed of dried ferns—
still only misplaced and never lost

so long as it's kept in mind, a part
of myself split along the grain and left
to watch over that corner of the world.

A Trout in the Well

*If you cannot keep earthworms and bugs out
of your well in any other way put a small trout
in the water. If your well is open to the sunlight,
as it should be, the fish will thrive amazingly.*
— *Farming, Volume 3, 1905*

No further from the sky than a lake bottom,
nor colder, nor any more dark—how far
does your thought move up the moss-softened rocks,
the cold meniscus of your mind climbing
the sheer bank of your landlocked pool toward
the distant halo?
                       At noon, the sun may dip
an angled ray into that shaft to mix
its inky silence with the brilliance
of your hidden scales, your spots of carmine
confined to their rings of blue, to wet
the west sky's canvas at dusk—clouds ruffled
in the likeness of stream water rushing.

For a New Roof

This will be the third roof I've had fastened to this house; the first
lasted over eighteen years, the second skin of shingles
only eleven before its jet edges cupped and curled
under the summer sun. Since this latest plating will outlast me,

I'm not sure why an old man should worry over just what brand
is written upon the sheaves arrayed in slabs along the peak,
or who should walk above me, roofing spade in hand, preparing
the high, angled field, as I will never witness the gravel's

gradual loosening, or see the shakes fishmouthed and lifted
by the wind, or watch the north face that's shaded by the ash tree
blossoming at last with moss and lichen. This almost seems

the sort of care you'd take when bundling up a loved one
to set them out alone into the night. But it's the house,
tucked beneath this roof from eave to eave, that will be staying put.

Elegy for a Sapling in Three Revelations

i.
That the cottonwood should have reached
that height in just three years' time,

stretching on its skin-smooth bark
as if the whole world were anxious

to watch it daub the canvas of the sky
with its fresh canopy blossoming.

ii.
That this tree should have grown nine feet
unnoticed by anyone within the care

of this cornered plot, except the finch
that flared amidst its chartreuse coins,

and marked the broadening of branch and bole
as it weaved its gold within its boughs.

iii.
How ruthless I have grown that *weed* should come
to mean not just the power to condemn,

but also now the license to ignore
the apology of beauty—the word's two halves

working in tandem like the lopper's
chiseled smile I brought out from the shed.

Abandoned Bicycle

In a windbreak between two corn fields,
a half mile from any house, it leans
against the tangle of a blowdown,
its geometry unmistakable.

Its reflectors shine like eyes in your headlights,
and the next morning finds it still upright,
as constant and as patient as a dog
ready for the next leg of some journey.

After three days, you wish that somebody
would just steal the thing, throw it in their truck
to give an end to this story, the suspense
being far more than a farm lane might manage.

The Natural History of Stones

"Nature is being everywhere reduced to a level."
—Pliny, The Natural History of Stones

I happen to know how this cobble
warming itself along the roadside ditch
came to lie among the spurge and coltsfoot:
Ellery Haskell's dump truck left it here
twelve years ago, contracted by the town,
his front end loader scraping the gray shape
of a wave into the mound of glacial
till at the far end of Snakeroot Road.

And eight thousand years before that, the stone
was hundreds of times this size, a razor-lipped
boulder chipped from the soil-scoured bedrock
far to the north and tumbled smooth, edges
deadened beneath a breathless crush of ice.

It was left steeped and sleeping in the shallow
lake that trailed the glacier in its retreat
until the ground rose, shifting the gravel mound
to where it lies today, and raising the earth
where Ellery's farmhouse stood—the same hill
he was mowing seven years ago,
when his tractor tipped and rolled upon him.

And I happen to know where the stone is found
that marks the place where Ellery lies,
for all the good that does him or me,
and for all this basking cobble cares.

A Cemetery in Greene, Maine

Slowed to a crawl by construction, we rolled
by the cemetery in our daily
commute processional. The road had grown
wider over time, closer to the headstones,
and I strained to read the inscriptions
on the first row of monuments as they passed.
And the markers, their limestone arches
rounded like the backs of chairs, were propped
in front of their long morning shadows,
lining the road to watch our parade.

Route 202, Heading North

The young moon asleep for hours,
tucked into the blue gauze of city glow
some twenty miles to the west, and what light
would fall from stars, loose and rattling
in their settings, is rinsed away by the headlights
pulling you along that gray thread of road.

Sweeping east past the blurred form of trees,
you see the tail lights of an 18-wheeler
floating red at the horizon's hinge.
In the night's cold math of rate and pace,
you'll overtake the rig in a few minute's time.

Alongside the semi, marker lights festoon
its broad and angled flank and make
a carnival booth in the right-hand lane—
orange and white bulbs carve a bright hollow
in the empty night. And for a moment,
engines hum in tandem, the miles fusing,
welded in the spectacle. But the highway
comes unraveled at last; time resumes,
and exiled from this momentary midway,
you go hurtling back into the darkness.

About the Author

Kevin Casey is the author of *And Waking...* (Bottom Dog Press, 2016) and *Ways to Make a Halo,* published by Aldrich Press in 2018. His poems have appeared in *Rust+Moth, Valparaiso Poetry Review, Connotation Press, Pretty Owl Poetry,* and Ted Kooser's syndicated column 'American Life in Poetry.'

Glass Lyre Press

exceptional works to replenish the spirit

Glass Lyre Press is an independent literary publisher interested in technically accomplished, stylistically distinct, and original work. Glass Lyre seeks diverse writers that possess a dynamic aesthetic and an ability to emotionally and intellectually engage a wide audience of readers.

Glass Lyre's vision is to connect the world through language and art. We hope to expand the scope of poetry and short fiction for the general reader through exceptionally well-written books, which evoke emotion, provide insight, and resonate with the human spirit.

Poetry Collections
Poetry Chapbooks
Select Short & Flash Fiction
Anthologies

www.GlassLyrePress.com

www.ingramcontent.com/pod-product-compliance
Lightning Source LLC
Chambersburg PA
CBHW021158080526
44588CB00008B/402